TEX
and Gloria

Written an

COLLINS COLOUR CUBS

COLLINS COLOUR CUBS

Tex the cowboy goes singing down the trail.

Home, Sandra home on the range...

We need some money, Gloria

Tex and Gloria think about food.

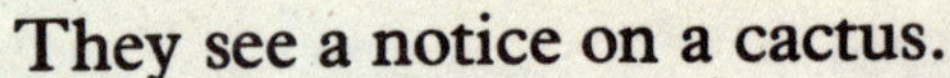

They see a notice on a cactus.

WANTED
DEAD OR ALIVE !!!
HANK BONES THE BAD
$50 REWARD

I hope we don't meet Hank Bones

Hee-
hee!

Hands up,
cowboy
YELP!

Give me your money - fast

I have no money

Give me your horse then

Oh dear

Hank leaps nimbly into the saddle

and gallops off.

At first Tex is sad.

Then he is angry.

Tex walks all day.

The sun is very hot.

But at last he finds
Bad Hank Bones.

Hands up, bad man

But . . .
Help!
Gloria!

Hee-hee, hard luck cowboy

GLORIA!

Gloria quickly sits on Hank.

They tie Hank up and . . .

take him to the sheriff.

You are a hero, Tex
Thanks, Sheriff
$

Tex and Gloria have
a very good dinner.

ISBN 0 00 123714 4
Printed in England